A Polar Bear Tale

by Xavier Floyd
illustrated by Judith Mitchell

Harcourt
SCHOOL PUBLISHERS

Printed in China

ISBN 10: 0-15-350679-2
ISBN 13: 978-0-15-350679-6

Ordering Options
ISBN 10: 0-15-350600-8 (Grade 3 On-Level Collection)
ISBN 13: 978-0-15-350600-0 (Grade 3 On-Level Collection)
ISBN 10: 0-15-357900-5 (package of 5)
ISBN 13: 978-0-15-357900-4 (package of 5)

1 2 3 4 5 6 7 8 9 10 985 12 11 10 09 08 07 06

In the far north, where the earth is covered in ice and snow, there lived a happy family. True, it was very cold, but the children loved to play in the wide-open white land. Suka and Nukka could slide across the ice. They could roll down the snowy slopes. They could laugh at floppy baby seals and playful white fox pups. They could imitate the penguins' funny walk. There was always plenty to do.

One cold, bright day, Mother called them away from their games. "Suka and Nukka, I need you to go to grandmother's house and bring her some fish," said Mother.

"Can't we please go later?" asked Suka. "We're busy playing."

"No," said Mother. "It will be too dark. Now go directly to grandmother's house. Do not stop to play. Do not talk to any strangers. If you do as I tell you, you will be home in plenty of time."

"Yes, Mother," they said. Then, reluctantly, they went on their way.

"Can't you go any faster, Nukka?" Suka asked as he jogged across the snow.

"No, Suka," gasped Nukka. She trailed behind Suka. "My legs are short. I'm going as fast as I can."

"We'll never get back home before dark," sighed Suka. "I wish there was a shortcut to grandmother's." They trudged past a mound of snow, feeling very sorry for themselves.

As soon as the children had passed the mound, it moved. It wasn't snow—it was a polar bear!

"I must get those children," thought Nanuq the polar bear. "If they see a bear, though, they will run away, so I need to trick them."

Nanuq snuck around Suka and Nukka so that they would not see him. Then he quickly dug a cave in the side of a large hill of snow, and he scurried inside and waited.

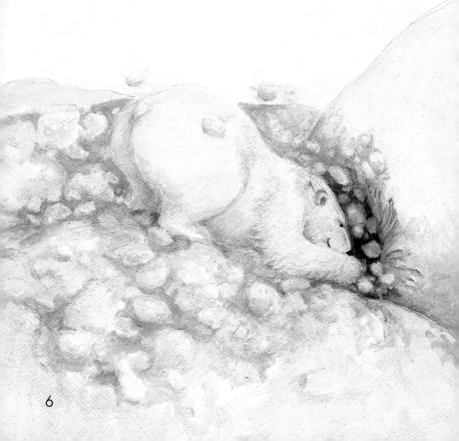

As the children walked past, Nanuq took a deep breath. Then he blew out with all his might. Suddenly, the children were surrounded by a whirling, swirling mass of snow.

"Suka, where are you?" cried Nukka.

"I'm here," Suka shouted.

Suka reached out and held onto his little sister's hand. Still, the mighty wind and snow blew them back and forth. Finally, it stopped.

Suka and Nukka looked around them at the new piles of snow. The great white land looked strange and unfamiliar.

"Which way is grandmother's house?" asked Nukka.

"I'm not sure," said Suka.

Suddenly, a voice called out. "Don't worry, I can help you. Come into my cave."

"Remember, we're not supposed to talk to strangers," whispered Suka.

The cunning bear was ready for this because he had heard them say each other's names. "I'm not really a stranger. I'm a friend of your grandmother's, Suka and Nukka. Now I wouldn't know your names if I were a stranger, would I?"

"That does make sense," whispered Nukka. "How else will we find our way?" They entered the cave and looked around, trying to see in the dark.

"I'm here, children," said Nanuq. "I'm very old and can't leave my bed. If you come close, I will draw you a map. Then you will be on your way to your dear grandmother's house."

Suka and Nukka followed the sound of the voice until they saw a large figure huddled in the shadows. They sat down next to it.

"Are you here, children?" asked the bear in a high, quavering voice.

"Yes," said Suka. He reached out and touched the hand of Grandmother's friend to let her know he was there. To Suka's horror, he felt soft fur and long, sharp claws.

"Friend of Grandmother, your hands are so soft and furry," said Suka.

"I am wearing warm gloves," said clever Nanuq. "I am old and feel the chilly air more than when I was young."

"I feel sharp nails, though," said Suka. "Are they part of your gloves?"

"Of course," replied Nanuq. "I need to be able to protect myself."

"I see," said Suka.

Just then, Nanuq moved a little. For a moment, his face moved into a tiny patch of light. Suka and Nukka both caught a glimpse of a long snout and sharp, white teeth. They looked at each other in horror—they were in a cave with a polar bear!

Suka thought quickly. "Dear friend, we are both very tired and hungry. Before you tell us how to get to Grandmother's house, we would like to rest and eat something. We have a lovely fish pie that we would be delighted to share with you."

Nanuq hesitated. The children were right there, but it was certainly hard to resist fish pie.

"I would love to try your pie," said Nanuq.

"Let us put together a nice bowl for you," suggested Suka.

He and Nukka backed away and opened their
basket. They took some of the fish out of the bowl
that Mother had packed. Then they dug through
the snow on the ground. They pulled out rocks
and chunks of thick ice, and they added them to
the bowl. Then they disguised the ice and rock
filling with mounds of tender fish.

"Here you are, friend of Grandmother," said
Suka. He handed the bowl to Nanuq.

The fish smell made the greedy bear's mouth
water. He eagerly took a big bite from the bowl.

Nanuq's teeth shattered like brittle glass as he bit into the hard rock and ice. He howled with pain and ran far away from the cave until he was out of sight.

Suka and Nukka found their way to grandmother's house, and they embraced her with all their might when she opened the door.

"We brought you some fish," said Nukka.

"How lovely!" cried Grandmother. "Would you like me to make a nice fish pie for you?"

Nukka and Suka looked at each other and cried, "No, thank you!

Think Critically

1. How is Nanuq the bear like the wolf in "Lon Po Po"? How is he different?

2. What does Suka and Nukka's mother tell them before they leave?

3. What does Nanuq do to get Suka and Nukka to trust him?

4. What probably happens to Nanuq after this story?

5. Do you think Suka and Nukka were wrong for going into the cave with Nanuq? Explain your answer.

 Language Arts

Poetry of the North Think about the place where Suka and Nukka live. Write a poem that describes their cold, snowy world.

 School-Home Connection Retell this story to a family member. Then discuss how it is alike and different from "Little Red Riding Hood."

Word Count: 975